W9-BTL-350

5-08

$23.95

AMERICAN WOMEN OF THE VIETNAM WAR

AMANDA FERGUSON

The Rosen Publishing Group, Inc., New York

With gratitude to Diane Carlson Evans, Kathy Fennel, Beth Marie Murphy, Susan O'Neill, Barbara Rozell, and Diana Sebek for sharing their experiences. Special thanks to Chris Banigan, who was not yet ready to fully speak about her personal experiences in Vietnam but provided invaluable support and information nevertheless.

Published in 2004 by The Rosen Publishing Group, Inc.
29 East 21st Street, New York, NY 10010

Library of Congress Cataloging-in-Publication Data

Ferguson, Amanda.
American women of the Vietnam War/by Amanda Ferguson.
    p. cm.—(American women at war)
Summary: Profiles American women who served as nurses and in other capacities during the Vietnamese Conflict, and describes different ways in which their experiences continue to be part of their lives.
Includes bibliographical references and index.
ISBN 0-8239-4448-4 (library binding)
1. Vietnamese Conflict, 1961–1975—Women—United States—Juvenile literature. 2. Vietnamese Conflict, 1961–1975—Biography—Juvenile literature. [1. Vietnamese Conflict, 1961–1975—Women. 2. Women and the military. 3. Women and war. 4. Women—Biography. 5. United States—Armed Forces—Women.]
I. Title. II. Series.
DS559.8.W6F47 2003
959.704'3'0820973—dc21

                                                        2003011572

Manufactured in the United States of America

On the front cover: U.S. Army nurses rest at Cam Ranh Bay in South Vietnam on July 14, 1965.
On the back cover: A caduceus, a symbol of the medical profession

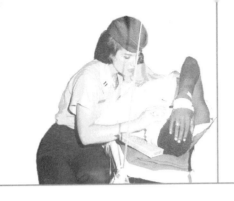

Contents

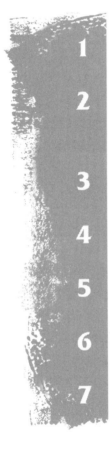

INTRODUCTION

Although their contributions have long been unrecognized, women have always played a part in U.S. military history. Women gathered intelligence and cared for the wounded. They also defended and maintained domestic property and industry in men's absence. Some even found ways to participate in direct combat. During the Revolutionary and Civil Wars, several women disguised themselves as men in order to fight on the battlefield. During World Wars I and II, thousands of women held noncombat positions such as

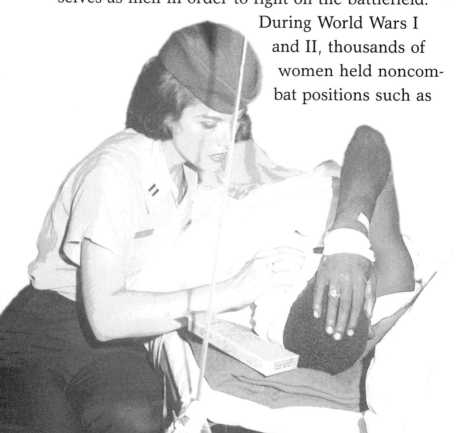

mechanics, spies, telephone operators, test pilots, clerks, and nurses. In theory, this allowed men who traditionally held these posts to serve on the battlefield. Many of these women sacrificed their personal safety in order to serve their country.

The U.S. Department of Defense kept no official records specifying the number of women who served in Vietnam. Most sources estimate that between 1962 and 1973, 7,000 to 12,000 women were assigned to active military duty in Vietnam. Most nurses served their standard one-year tour of duty between 1969 and 1971. This period represented the greatest number of U.S. troops stationed in Vietnam. The majority of nurses worked in surgical facilities, field hospitals, and medical evacuation centers. Others worked as military intelligence officers, translators, clerks, and flight controllers. In addition to those who served in the military, more than 20,000 civilian women, including journalists, teachers, and humanitarians, served in Vietnam. Civilians worked independently or with organizations such as the Red Cross.

All of these women served voluntarily. In the late 1960s, professional opportunities for women in the United States were largely limited to teaching

Learning how to operate tanks and jeeps was one of the many challenges faced by members of the WAC (Women's Army Corps). In Vietnam, few women were given the opportunity to take active roles in combat. Most served as nurses, translators, reporters, and stenographers.

and nursing jobs. For some, serving in Vietnam offered adventure and experience unavailable in the United States. Some volunteered out of a sense of social obligation. Others were lured by the military's offer to pay for their education.

After World War II, it seemed that Vietnam would finally achieve independence after hundreds of years of foreign occupation. Most recently, France and Japan had ruled Vietnam. But France wanted to take back its former colony. At first, the United States was in favor of Vietnam's independence. But the United States knew that Vietnam's leader, Ho Chi Minh, was a Communist. It believed that if Ho Chi Minh turned Vietnam into a Communist nation, other Southeast Asian countries would follow suit. With this in mind, the United States supported France's efforts to regain control of Vietnam. The United States gave France millions of dollars to fight Ho Chi Minh's army.

France suffered major defeats against Ho Chi Minh's army. In 1954, France pulled out of Vietnam. The United States helped arrange the division of Vietnam: Ho Chi Minh would govern North Vietnam, and Ngo Dinh Diem, an anti-Communist, would govern South Vietnam. Elections would be held in 1956 to reunite the country under one regime. When it became clear that the Vietnamese population would favor North Vietnam's Communist regime, Ngo Dinh Diem, with U.S. diplomatic support, cancelled the election. Vietnamese Communist sympathizers, known as the Vietcong (VC), began raising a guerrilla army to overthrow the South Vietnamese government. Over the next few years, the United States sent thousands of military advisors and troops to support the South

Wounded soldiers are quickly transferred to an ambulance bound for a medical facility in South Vietnam. Although 58,000 Americans died in the Vietnam War, many more were saved because of advancements in medicine and knowledgeable nurses and doctors.

Vietnamese government. By 1965, the United States was officially at war with North Vietnam.

By 1969, more than half a million U.S. troops were stationed in Vietnam. With more soldiers came more fighting and a greater need for nurses. The casualties were horrific. For the first time, helicopters were used to quickly transport casualties to hospitals. Injuries that would have killed a man in a previous war—men literally blown to pieces—were treated on a regular basis.

The last U.S. troops left Vietnam in 1972. The United States had not achieved its political objectives. Many viewed the war as a complete and unnecessary waste. With little public or government support, Vietnam veterans were left to deal with the physical, emotional, and social consequences of their service.

The biographies presented here are not intended to represent the Vietnam War experience. Rather, six women explain what the Vietnam War was like for them personally: why they chose to go to Vietnam, what they experienced there, and how those experiences affected them.

KATHY FENNEL, ARMY NURSE CORPS (VIETNAM, 1968–1969)

Kathy Fennel would have preferred to go to Vietnam with Dr. Tom Dooley. In the 1950s, Dooley established clinics and hospitals through-out Southeast Asia. These facilities treated more than half a million people for illnesses such as smallpox, leprosy, malnutrition, and malaria. Dooley wrote several books about his experiences. The governments of both the United States and South Vietnam recognized Dooley for his work. Although Dooley died in 1961, Fennel was inspired to provide similar

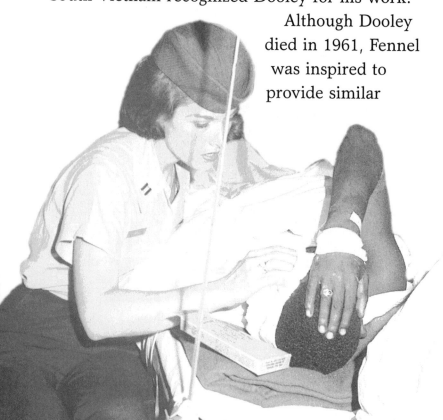

humanitarian assistance in Vietnam. While she was in nursing school, it became apparent that if she wanted to be a nurse in Vietnam, it would likely have to be done for the military. Taking advantage of her operating room experience, Fennel enlisted in the army and requested an operating room assignment in Vietnam.

As well as being a skilled and dedicated doctor, Tom Dooley also wrote three memoirs about his experiences in Vietnam: *Deliver Us From Evil*, *The Edge of Tomorrow*, and *The Night They Burned the Mountain*. Upon his death in 1961, Dooley was reviewed for sainthood by the Catholic Church but was denied canonization.

TET OFFENSIVE

Traditionally, military forces recognized a truce over Tet, the Vietnamese holiday celebrating the lunar New Year. The Vietnamese spend the holiday tending graves and paying tribute to their ancestors. On the eve of Tet in 1968, the Vietcong launched a major attack against U.S. and South Vietnamese forces in more than 100 towns and cities. The Vietcong even attacked the U.S. Embassy in Saigon, killing five marines. Although the offensive was technically a defeat for the Vietcong— 37,000 Vietcong soldiers were killed, compared to 2,500 American casualties, and U.S. troops overtook every city that had been captured—it proved that the U.S. government and military had miscalculated the Vietcong's strength and ability. The Tet Offensive shook the confidence of the American public, which had been told that a U.S. victory was close at hand.

Fennel arrived in Vietnam shortly after the Tet Offensive. Tet is the Vietnamese New Year, based on the lunar calendar. In late January 1968, North

Vietnamese troops assaulted U.S. forces throughout Vietnam during Tet.

Fennel was assigned to work at the 12th Evacuation Hospital in Cu Chi, a province about 30 miles (48 kilometers) northwest of Saigon. Sandwiched between Saigon and the Cambodian border, the hospital was in an area where heavy fighting happened. Most of the buildings on the

Members of the U.S. military police take cover as two American soldiers lie dead at the gate of the U.S. Embassy on January 31, 1968. During the Tet Offensive, the U.S. Embassy was one of the first places besieged by Vietcong guerrillas.

CU CHI TUNNELS

Between 1945 and 1975, more than 75 miles (121 km) of multilevel underground tunnels and chambers were carved

A man at the base of a narrow Cu Chi tunnel

beneath Saigon and the surrounding Cu Chi province. Built during France's occupation, the tunnels were expanded during the Vietnam War. The intricate network housed an entire community. It included meeting rooms, kitchens, sleeping quarters, schools, and hospitals. The Vietcong used the tunnels to plan and execute attacks against U.S. and South Vietnamese forces. Thousands of Vietnamese civilians took shelter in the tunnels during U.S. bombings. U.S. forces made several attempts to clear the tunnels. Cu Chi became one of the most heavily bombed and defoliated sites in Vietnam. Despite these efforts, the tunnels remained largely intact for the duration of the war. The tunnels have come to symbolize the endurance and ingenuity of the Vietnamese people. Today, the tunnels' entrances have been widened to accommodate curious tourists.

---

hospital compound were Quonset huts that did little to keep out the heavy rains during monsoon (the rainy) season. During the dry season, the wind blew sand everywhere, making it difficult to keep wounds clean. When Fennel wasn't on duty, she spent time in her hooch (tent), reading, listening to music, and catching up on sleep.

After her first month in Vietnam, the twenty-three-year-old began to question the U.S. government's honesty about the war. The numbers of officially reported casualties did not match what she was seeing. "And we were only one small hospital," she notes. "It seemed to me that we weren't winning, that something was wrong. I didn't know what that was, but you couldn't look at that kind of trauma and still believe it made sense."[1]

Fennel had little time to resolve these questions; she had too many patients to care for, both American *and* Vietnamese. Under the principles of the Geneva Conventions and the Hippocratic oath, all patients had to receive humane medical treatment. This included prisoners of war, of course. This proved difficult for some American medical staff and wounded GIs. Sometimes staff and wounded Americans directed their anger and frustration over the war toward Vietnamese patients.

"There were times that I had resentments," Fennel admits. "I'd think, 'I'm tired; I don't want to get up and take care of Vietnamese patients, because in a few hours I have to do it again for Americans.' We all had those feelings, but we were young and exhausted. We didn't understand."[2] The close proximity of Vietnamese and American wounded sometimes had more positive effects; recuperating patients sometimes gained respect and compassion for each other as fellow soldiers who suffered similar injuries.

Shortages of equipment and staff—and the severity of conditions—forced the hospital staff to be creative. Fennel notes that the hard work and experimental surgery and treatment done in Vietnam later led to important medical advances.

GENEVA CONVENTIONS

After World War II (1938–1945), world leaders met in Geneva, Switzerland, and negotiated the Geneva Conventions on the Laws of War. The Geneva Conventions require that all civilians and prisoners of war be treated humanely. During the Vietnam War, U.S. military stationed in Vietnam were given handouts reminding them of these obligations. One such handout read:

> As a member of the US military forces, you will comply with the Geneva Prisoner of War Conventions of 1949 to which your country adheres. Under these conventions . . . YOU CANNOT AND MUST NOT: Mistreat your prisoner; Humiliate or degrade him; Take any of his personal effects which do not have significant military value; Refuse him medical treatment if required and available. ALWAYS TREAT YOUR PRISONER HUMANELY.[3]
>
> —*From* The Enemy in Your Hands,
> *Military Assistance Command, Vietnam*

In particular, many important advances in artery
and blood vessel work were made thanks to the
efforts of military doctors and nurses to save the
limbs of wounded soldiers.

In addition to medical work, nurses provided
solace and spiritual comfort. Patients often turned
to nurses for a final moment of emotional contact.
To them, nurses represented the mothers, girlfriends, or wives they would never see again.
Although it was difficult to cope with such
moments, nurses understood how vital it was that
patients not die alone. Fennel is haunted by the
memory of a young GI who had been in a mine
accident. Shot through his stomach, the man's
entire buttocks had been blown away; he was
dying. "He grabbed my hand and wouldn't let go,"
she remembers. "He was married, a young kid. He
was like Godzilla, he was so strong. I tried to pry
his fingers off because his wedding ring was hurt-
ing my hand. He turned to me and screamed
'Henrietta!' At that moment, I was as good as
Henrietta. He knew he was dying. I could feel him
totally relaxing as if he were melting. He was pro-
nounced dead. They took off the tubes, and I was
left to get him off the table. We had thirty more
patients to deal with. I couldn't believe that I was

talking to this kid and he was alive and strong,
even though he was bleeding out everywhere. And
then he was dead."[4]

Sometimes, nurses were left to deal with emotionally charged situations because no one else
would. Fennel remembers once when a U.S. helicopter pilot asked the hospital to tend to a young
Vietnamese woman. In order to get the hospital to
admit her, he said that the woman had been shot in
the stomach. As it turned out, the woman wasn't
wounded; she was in labor, three months before
the baby was due. A doctor on staff specialized in
delivering babies back in the States. He wasn't willing to get out of bed to help in the delivery. He
wanted to preserve his strength for the next round
of incoming wounded soldiers.

Fennel was ordered to deliver the baby. The
situation was hopeless. Even in ideal conditions,
without the advanced medical technology and
equipment that is available today, premature
babies had little chance of survival. Fennel was
ordered to help the woman as best she could.
"What I was seeing was the terminal moment," she
says. "All the men had left. Nobody wanted to deal
with it. Eventually, it's always the patient and the
nurse. I remember seeing the baby's corpse in the

basin and thinking, this shouldn't be happening."[5] The event came to symbolize the war for Fennel; the images from that day continue to haunt her.

The daily grind was depressing. Fennel coped with her depression by spending time with friends. Although she was a ranking officer, the hospital staff generally ignored rules forbidding fraternization between officers and nonranking military. "We got yelled at for doing it, but the people who worked in the operation room [OR] would do things together, even if it was just sit in the OR and talk. If you were down, they helped you get back up; if they were down, you helped them. It was the only way to stay sane."[6]

Fennel left Vietnam a few months earlier than she had intended. A swimming accident left her with a serious neck injury. She was sent to the United States on medical evacuation. She spent the remainder of her service recuperating at the Valley Forge General Hospital in Pennsylvania. Gradually, she switched from recovering patient to part-time operating nurse. She was discharged from the Army Nurse Corps in 1969.

In 1971, she married another Vietnam veteran, a former army medic. Over the next decade, the couple began raising a family. She worried about the chances of her children developing health problems as a result of the Agent Orange she'd been exposed to in Vietnam. From 1961 to 1971, the U.S. Air Force sprayed millions of gallons of the highly toxic chemical in order to destroy forests where Vietcong (VC) troops might be hiding, as well as to destroy crops that might be providing the VC army with food. Agent Orange has since been identified as the cause of many serious health problems, including cancer, diabetes, and birth defects.

Fennel also made sure she was tested for hepatitis C, a blood-borne disease she risked contracting, because in Vietnam her hands were immersed in blood without rubber gloves. Eventually, she returned to school to become a physician's aide, a job that allows her to work closely with doctors.

First Lieutenant Sharon Lane was the only American servicewoman in Vietnam who was killed by enemy fire. Lane was decorated with many medals, including the Purple Heart, a combat decoration awarded to soldiers who are wounded or killed in the act of serving their country during wartime.

BORN TO HONOR
EVER AT PEACE
LT SHARON A LANE
U.S. ARMY NURSE CORPS
KILLED IN VIET NAM
JUNE 8 1969

A statue of a proud Sharon Lane stands at the entranceway of Aultman Hospital in Canton, Ohio. Lane was admired for her courage in wartime as well as her compassion toward all patients, including Vietnamese soldiers and prisoners of war.

In 1993, Fennel and her husband returned to Vietnam with Operation Smile, a volunteer organization group that funds and coordinates cleft lip and palate surgery in developing countries. During her flight to Da Nang, she read a biography about Sharon Ann Lane, a nurse who was killed during a mortar attack on the 312th Evacuation Hospital in Chu Lai. She was touched by the fact that

Lane had volunteered to work in the Vietnamese ward. It was an assignment that most nurses took with reluctance. Lane worked hard to treat her patients with compassion, no matter what side they were fighting on. With the blessing of Lane's mother, Fennel established the Sharon Ann Lane Foundation in honor of the young nurse's legacy. The foundation worked to build and fund a medical clinic in Chu Lai, dedicated to the memory of Sharon Ann Lane and the children of Vietnam. Currently, the foundation is working with the Hue Medical School in Hue, Vietnam's former imperial capital, to establish a medical educational exchange program. Fennel returns to Vietnam from time to time to help with the program.

Fennel's present work with the clinic helps her come to terms with her former experiences in Vietnam. "I didn't have a lot of time to play with Vietnamese children during the war," she explains. "I do now. There is a beauty in what's happening here. Now we're involved with working towards a present and a future."[7]

BARBARA ROZELL, U.S. AGENCY FOR INTERNATIONAL DEVELOPMENT (VIETNAM, 1968)

Barbara Rozell was disturbed by the graphic images of the Vietnam War shown on the evening news. Rozell is the daughter of an army colonel and was part of San Francisco's counterculture in the 1960s. Her friends and family often had strong and opposing points of view about the war. "It was so big at the universities to be antiwar, antigovernment, burn the flag," she says. "That just went against my core values as the daughter of a military officer whose way of life had always

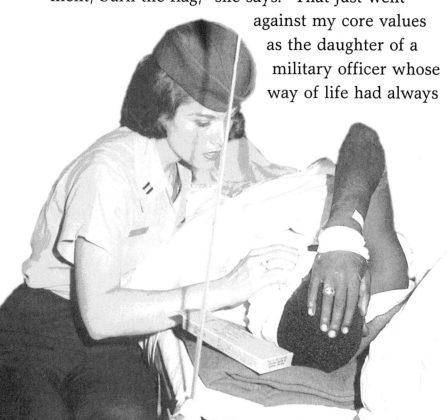

been country first, family second, and yourself third. I had this need to go over and figure out for myself whether or not we should be there."[1]

She saw an ad in the paper announcing that the United States Agency for International Development (USAID) was seeking administrative staff to work in Vietnam. The agency was an independent government agency under the U.S. State Department. Its duties were to coordinate humanitarian relief

While American troops fought overseas in Vietnam, social and cultural revolution took hold at home. Many college students rallied against the Vietnam War as well as other domestic issues, including racial and gender inequality.

projects, such as building schools, sending teachers and doctors to villages, and sending agricultural specialists to help replant crops destroyed in war. Working for USAID seemed to Rozell like a good way to both serve the U.S. government and work toward principles of peace.

It took six months for Rozell to process the necessary paperwork and security clearances. In January 1968, she went to Washington, D.C., for a month of orientation. Her orientation included a brief introduction to Vietnamese culture, language, and economics. She also received an overview of the agency's mission. Shortly afterward, she was on her way to Vietnam.

The flight to Saigon was long. Rozell and two other USAID colleagues decided to stop in Hong Kong for the night. They wanted to be fresh when they arrived in Saigon. The next morning, they waited to board their flight. Hours went by. What was the holdup? Rumors flew: an enormous VC offensive had taken place; the VC had taken over Saigon; the VC had taken over all airports. As it turns out, the women had arrived in the middle of the Tet Offensive.

With no money, work, or official orders, Rozell began her war experience stuck in Hong Kong until further notice. She contacted the U.S. consulate in Hong Kong for advice. They told her that the only thing they could do to help was to bail her out of jail in case the manager of her hotel decided to arrest her for not being able to pay her hotel bill. After several days of waiting for further instruction, a U.S. officer told her that there would be a military flight to Saigon the next morning; if there were any empty seats available, there was a possibility that they would take civilians. The same afternoon, word came from Washington, D.C., that the situation in Vietnam was very dangerous. If she wanted, the agency would assign her to a different post. Despite the risks involved, Barbara decided to go to Saigon. "I don't think I was scared," she says. "At twenty-two, you feel infallible."[2]

The Tet Offensive was still going on when she arrived in Saigon. Curfews were in effect, and the threat of terrorism was high. Vietnamese civilians were not allowed to go to their jobs at U.S. government agencies. Gradually, curfews eased and Vietnamese employees were allowed to return to work.

Rozell worked for a USAID program division manager. USAID aimed to earn the trust and loyalty of the Vietnamese population through

USAID took on the responsibility of providing basic health care for Vietnamese civilians during the war. Pictured above, a U.S. Navy corpsman administers a cholera inoculation to a young man who survived a massive flood.

public works programs. USAID field workers performed such tasks as setting up water systems, schools, and health clinics and bringing electricity to small villages. They were required to send progress reports to USAID program officers in Saigon. The program officers coordinated the field workers' activities, estimated program costs, and prepared budget reports that would be put before Congress for approval in the national budget. Rozell's job was to help prepare these reports.

Two months into her stay, Rozell began to feel that the goals of the USAID program were at cross-purposes with the military. What good was it for the U.S. government to fund public works projects in local villages when those villages might be bombed by the U.S. military? Who, then, was the enemy? One night, she sat on the roof of her hotel, looking out over the river onto a little jungle area. "I looked up and saw two jets circling on either side," she remembers. "One would swoop down and drop some kind of bomb—you'd see this amazing explosion of light and smoke. As soon as he finished his arc, the one from the other side would come down and do the same thing. At the same time, choppers came in and dropped a bunch of soldiers who ran into the jungle. I could hear the machine gun fire and see little puffs of smoke, maybe from grenades. A little while later, they all came running out of the jungle. Some guys got picked up by gunships. Some guys were on stretchers and got picked up by medical helicopters. Then they were gone. So now did we own the jungle? Did the VC own the jungle? I began to think, you know, this just doesn't feel right. Why are we doing this?"[3]

During a raid, U.S. Marines jump from their helicopters into tall marshland grasses in pursuit of Vietcong guerrilla bands. Unaccustomed to the climate and vegetation of Southeast Asia, American soldiers had to quickly adapt to their surroundings.

She also became aware that many U.S. civilians and military personnel living in Saigon did not respect the South Vietnamese military, whom they were supposedly supporting. "We called the Vietnamese military White Mice. We didn't have a lot of faith in them,"[4] she recalls. She says that curfews set by the South Vietnamese government and military were frequently ignored. "I went across a bridge in a Jeep one time with a guy. A South

Vietnamese soldier told us to stop. We ignored him and drove right on our merry way,"[5] she says.

When her eighteen-month assignment in Saigon was over, Rozell decided to leave Vietnam. She felt she had done her job as best she could. Staying would serve no further purpose. "I didn't want to be a war groupie,"[6] she says. She considered working for USAID in Turkey. But it occurred to her that she did not want to live in another country where she would be working and living in an isolated American community. "I was having dinner with some of my cohorts, and I started to listen to the conversation around me," she explains. "People were saying, 'I can't find any good servants,' 'We can't get any fresh meat at the commissary,' and 'Liquor's really getting expensive.' I'd heard this conversation too many times. I could go to Turkey and hear the same conversation; it wouldn't make any difference what country I was in."[7]

In 1969, Rozell returned to San Francisco. The antiwar movement had now turned explosive. She became guarded when talking about her experiences in Vietnam and eventually avoided the subject all together. "If you even mentioned the word 'Vietnam', you had no idea what kind of

WINNING HEARTS AND MINDS

"The U.S. military had been preceded by years of attempts to rebuild the country via the United States Agency for International Development (USAID) and other organizations . . . South Vietnam's people would have to be won over 'village by village, hut by hut, by social and political means, with information and propaganda' . . . Americans with both the military and USAID and the Volunteers of America and many other organizations risked their lives every day, not only building roads and schools but digging wells, giving shots, mending cleft palates, teaching hygiene. They organized elections under sometimes terrifying conditions of atrocious intimidation by both the Vietcong and the Republic of Vietnam itself . . . None of it worked . . . Nonetheless, these attempts at political, agrarian and economic reform were no mere window-dressing. They were accomplished by earnest, dedicated men and women at an enormous cost . . . "[8]

—*John Berthesel, correspondent in Vietnam for* Newsweek *magazine, 1966–1967* response you were going to get. My stomach would turn in knots. I knew that people would discount what I had done or would turn and literally walk away. They didn't want to hear about personal experiences; it was too raw."[9]

While in San Francisco, Rozell reconnected with a former boyfriend. They soon married. When the couple began raising a family, she didn't work much outside of the home. She sometimes wonders what life would have been like if she'd continued working for the State Department. Ultimately, though, she's happy with the life and the adventures she's had with her family.

In 1995, Rozell decided to go on a tour of Vietnam with a group of women who had served there in various capacities. Connie Stevens, a performer who entertained U.S. troops in Vietnam 1969 and 1970, filmed the trip for a documentary, *A Healing*. The chance to talk with others who had had similar experiences helped put Rozell's time in Vietnam into perspective. She has since shown the film at several schools, using it as a springboard to talk about the Vietnam War. The film has even helped her share her experiences with those closest to her.

A crowd of 20,000 troops listens intently as Connie Stevens sings at the annual Bob Hope Christmas Show in Vietnam in December 1969. At Christmastime, musical acts and other varieties of entertainment were provided in hopes of lifting soldiers' spirits.

She was particularly surprised by her son's rapt interest in the documentary; she had thought that, since he already knew about her service, the three-hour film might be dull for him. Instead, it sharpened his appreciation for what his mother had gone through. "A number of times it brought tears to his eyes," she says. "When it was finished, he said 'Mom, those women were amazing. I would love to meet those women.'"[10]

DIANE CARLSON EVANS, ARMY NURSE CORPS (VIETNAM, 1968–1969)

When their son was drafted in 1966, Mr. and Mrs. Carlson were extremely worried that he would be sent into active combat duty in Vietnam. When he instead received orders to go to Korea, they were relieved. They never imagined, then, that they would have to worry about their *daughter* serving in Vietnam.

Diane Carlson grew up in Minnesota. She followed the war in Vietnam with great interest. Her roommate at nursing school had spent a year in Vietnam. She told Carlson how

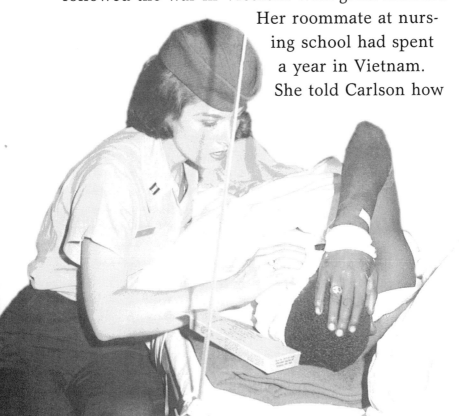

Elizabeth Hosington (*left*) and Anna Mae Hays proudly stand at the Pentagon in Washington, D.C., where they were nominated as the first female generals in the United States by President Nixon.

desperate the military was to recruit nurses. Carlson wanted to practice her nursing skills where they were most needed. So, she went to an army recruiter to find out how to join. The fact that the Army Nurse Corps would pay for her senior year at nursing school was a benefit. When she told her parents that she had enlisted, they were stunned.

Carlson was not the first woman in her family to serve in the military. Her aunt had risen through the ranks in the Women's Army Corps during World War II and had earned a doctorate degree under the GI Bill (a law giving money to returning GIs for education). She told Carlson that if it hadn't been for the military, she would not have had those opportunities.

Carlson did not tell many of her friends or classmates that she had volunteered to serve in the increasingly unpopular war. Those she did tell questioned her decision. They told her that she didn't seem like the type. At the time, many people assumed that women who joined the military were masculine or unattractive, unable to find a husband and lead a "normal" civilian life.

Undaunted, Carlson went to Fort Sam Houston, in Texas, for six weeks of basic training. She also had some field training at Camp Bullus, where she learned to pitch tents and set up gurneys (wheeled stretchers) and field hospitals. None of this prepared her for what she would face in Vietnam. Looking back, she is resentful that the military did not prepare her for combat: "I think that it was a stereotype: women are the weaker sex so we won't train them; we won't give them weapons to protect themselves with because the men will protect them. Well, if they were going to send us into a combat zone, which they did, we should have been trained to protect ourselves. We should have been able to carry a gun if we needed one. Our training should have been more in depth, and we should have learned how to take care of each other during times of mass casualties and tragedy."[1]

Carlson spent the first half of her tour of duty at the 36th Evacuation Hospital, a surgical and rehabilitation hospital, in Vung Tau in South Vietnam. Most of the arriving patients had been treated at other hospitals and came to Vung Tau for delayed surgery. Their wounds had already been cleaned, and they arrived in clean blue pajamas. Carlson wanted to go farther north, closer to the fighting and closer to where the wounded were coming in. She requested a transfer and was sent to the 71st Evacuation Hospital at Pleiku, close to the Cambodian border.

Carlson got her wish. The 71st EVAC was in one of the highest combat zones in Vietnam. Helicopters delivered wounded men from fields that were minutes away from the hospital. Sometimes casualties arrived fifty at a time. It was difficult, but necessary, to determine which patients would be treated first—staff and supplies were limited. "That's where a lot of guilt came in," she says. "If we'd only had more supplies, more doctors, more nurses; if this patient wouldn't have had to wait three hours for surgery, maybe he would have survived. Yet we could only do what we could."[2]

Carlson wrote home but was unable to describe the reality of her work. Years later, she had a chance

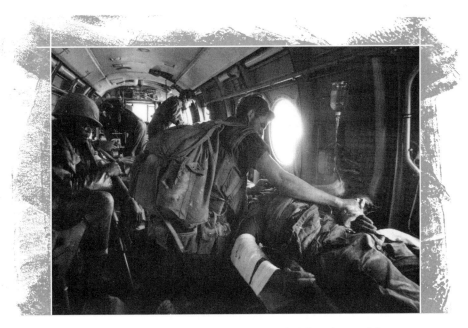

An air ambulance, full of the bodies of wounded American soldiers, flies over Vietnam to safety. The Vietnam War was the longest military conflict in United States history. About 58,000 soldiers lost their lives and 304,000 were wounded in combat.

to read the letters she'd sent her parents. "When I read those letters, I sat there in shock. If they hadn't been in my own handwriting, I wouldn't have believed I'd written them."[3] Because she hadn't wanted her parents to worry, Carlson had written about the weather, friends, and parties— anything besides the war. Every once in a while, though, a detail would slip out. "I would write something like, 'Oh, we were rocketed last night,' but then I'd end everything with, 'Don't worry about me, I'm fine.'"[4] She also had trouble admitting to herself what she was experiencing: "I started a diary in Vietnam and quit writing in it. I decided I didn't want to remember any of this stuff, so why write it down?"[5]

When her tour of duty ended, Carlson returned to Minnesota. She found that many stereotypes about women in the military remained unchanged. On her first day of work at the North Memorial Hospital in Minneapolis, the head nurse was skeptical that Carlson had actually served in Vietnam: "First she looked at my feet, and then every inch of me up from there. Finally she sneered, 'You don't look like you've been in the military.' I thought, what am I supposed to look like?"[6]

The routine responsibilities at the civilian hospital were unsatisfying in comparison to the challenges of combat nursing. She had trouble comforting patients who suffered from relatively minor aches and pains. After the challenges and freedoms she'd experienced as a combat nurse, the new bureaucracy and professional protocol she was expected to adhere to felt stifling. She decided to return to the military and was sent to Fort Sam Houston, where she was appointed head nurse in the surgical intensive care unit, treating wounded soldiers returning from combat. "In a way, I was right back in Vietnam," she explains. "I was taking care of the soldiers again, and I was really happy doing that."[7]

In Vietnam, she had never had time to talk to her patients or care for them after their initial treatment. In Texas, she was able to spend time with patients. Working with veterans helped her process her own Vietnam experiences and adjust to civilian life. At the same time, the opportunity to know her patients better was challenging. In Vietnam, she only had time to deal with patients' initial physical injuries. Now, she watched soldiers and their loved ones deal with the longer-term consequences of those injuries: "I had to talk to the families and

Vietnam veterans place mementos on the Vietnam Women's Memorial during its dedication ceremony on November 11, 1993. Thousands of veterans attended the dedication of the memorial, which honors more than 11,000 women who served in Vietnam.

prepare them for what they were going to see when they went into the intensive care unit, that their son or fiancé had lost both his legs and both his arms in Vietnam. It was very stressful to see how traumatic this was for the families."[8]

While working at the Veterans Administration, she met her future husband. In 1972, the couple decided to start a family. When she learned she was pregnant, Carlson left the military but continued to nurse part-time. In 1980, with four children to care for, she quit nursing altogether. For many years, she tried to forget her experiences in Vietnam; the memories were too painful. After Carlson went to Washington, D.C., for the dedication of the Vietnam Veterans

POST-TRAUMATIC STRESS DISORDER

Post-traumatic stress disorder (PTSD) is a combination of responses to a traumatic event outside the normal range of human experience. *The Diagnostic and Statistical Manual of Mental Disorders* notes that the most common traumas that cause PTSD include a serious threat to one's life or the lives of loved ones; "sudden destruction of one's home or community"; and "seeing someone who has been, or is being, seriously injured or killed." The majority of those who served in Vietnam experienced one or more of these traumas, some on a daily basis. Symptoms include involuntary "re-experiencing"[9] of the trauma, such as flashbacks; avoidance of things associated with the trauma, manifested as amnesia; and hyper-arousal, unpredictable, and often violent, outbursts. Many vets suffered from PTSD without knowing it. Some tried to manage its symptoms with drugs and alcohol; some thought—and were told—that they were crazy. PTSD is now recognized as a normal response to extreme trauma.

A statue at the Vietnam Women's Memorial in Washington, D.C., depicts the invaluable care and bravery of the women who served in a devastating war. The statue was dedicated in 1993.

Memorial in 1982, she found herself thinking about her time in Vietnam.

She sought out other female veterans and discovered that, like her, many had never talked about their experiences. In 1983, she founded the Vietnam Women's Memorial Project, which

VIETNAM WOMEN'S MEMORIAL PROJECT

Members of the Vietnam Women's Memorial Project struggled for permission to place the monument on the National Mall in Washington, D.C., near the Vietnam Veterans Memorial. In 1988, Diane Carlson Evans spoke to a number of national veterans' service organizations and requested their legislative support: "We wish to stand near the Wall of names of those we cared for in death and the bronze statue portraying those we helped come home. We were with them in war and we want to be with them now. I want the women who served to know that they are not forgotten, that there's a special place for them, too, on honored ground."[10]

sought to identify and honor civilian and military women who had served in Vietnam and to educate the public about their role in history. The organization was also dedicated to promoting research of service-related health issues, including post-traumatic stress disorder (PTSD) and the effects of Agent Orange.

It took ten years to raise the funding and support to create the memorial. On November 11, 1993, the Vietnam Women's Memorial was dedicated as part of the Vietnam Veterans Memorial. Located in Washington, D.C., a few yards away from the Wall (as the Vietnam Veterans Memorial is called), the memorial features a bronze sculpture by artist Glenna Goodacre of three female Vietnam veterans, one of whom tends a wounded soldier.

BETH MARIE MURPHY, NAVY NURSE CORPS (VIETNAM, 1969–1970)

When Beth Marie Murphy told her parents she had enlisted in the navy, they were not happy. She held firm against their objections. The idea of being able to serve her country and travel the world at the same time appealed to Murphy, who had never been out of her home state of Massachusetts.

After graduating from nursing school, Murphy was assigned to work in a military hospital in the United States. One day, army officers made rounds asking nurses to volunteer to go to Vietnam. She didn't know much about the

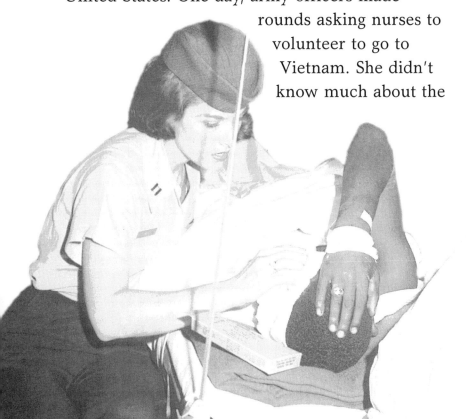

situation in Vietnam, other than the fact that
there was fighting. Inspired by her roommate's
father, a marine, Murphy decided to enlist with
the Navy Nurse Corps. She did so primarily
because navy nurses cared for marines and
also because she liked the navy recruiter better
than the army recruiter.

Murphy had six weeks of naval nursing training at a base in Rhode Island. Training consisted
primarily of learning to how to march and salute,
how to wear a uniform properly, and how to
jump off a ship into the ocean. Although she had
been told that it was unlikely that she would be
sent to Vietnam for at least two years, within
three months she received orders to go there. In
order not to upset her parents, she didn't tell
them she would be serving in Vietnam until the
day before she left.

Assigned to work on the USS *Sanctuary*,
twenty-two-year-old Murphy figured she would be
safe on the ship. When she arrived at the airport
in Da Nang, there was no one to meet her or tell
her where she was supposed to go. Two men
offered to drive her to the U.S. Naval Hospital in
Da Nang. There, they told her, she could find
transportation to the ship. As they made their way
to the hospital, something blew up directly behind

their jeep. "All of a sudden, I realized I could really get hurt,"[1] she recalls.

Hovering about a mile (1.6 km) off of the Vietnamese coast in the South China Sea, the USS *Sanctuary* was a large multideck hospital with a staff of 750. The boat traveled up and down the Vietnamese coast, servicing the area between Da Nang and the demilitarized zone, where most

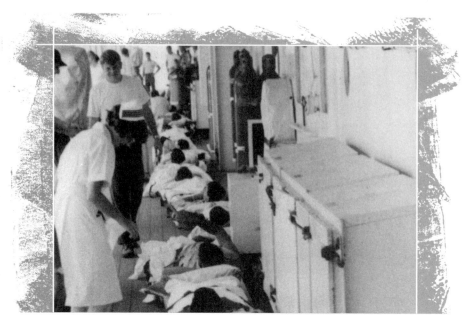

A navy nurse attends the sick and wounded on stretchers on the deck of the hospital ship USS *Sanctuary* (AH-17) moored in Da Nang Harbor in April 1970. The men have just arrived by a medical evacuation helicopter. Hospital ships were an integral part of medical operations during the Vietnam War. Tens of thousands of patients received care on several ships used for such purposes.

VIETNAMESE WOMEN SOLDIERS

Popular culture has reduced the wartime images of Vietnamese women to those of helpless victims, prostitutes, or abandoned war brides. The social reality was much more complex. An estimated 200,000 highly skilled and trained women served in the North Vietnamese and Vietcong armies. They operated underground communications networks, ran weapons depots, and commanded platoons of soldiers. They also ran intelligence operations and clinics throughout the jungles. They shot at American planes and captured American

A female soldier from North Vietnam stands guard in a field.

POWs; they buried the dead, nursed the wounded, and worked to keep agricultural and industrial production at prewar levels. Their participation played a large part in North Vietnam's ultimate victory.

marines were stationed. Helicopters flew most patients to the ship directly from the battlefield. Occasionally, small Vietnamese boats would deliver sick and injured patients. This turned out to be dangerous, Murphy learned. There was always a chance that a mother begging doctors to take her child aboard might be a Vietcong soldier waiting for a chance to launch a grenade. Despite the risk of terrorism, Murphy remembers that the gangplank was always lowered. As it turns out, U.S. soldiers who forgot to unload their live ammunition before they boarded posed a greater threat to the ship's security.

Without the dirt and dust that plagued most field hospitals, doctors and nurses could perform more complicated surgeries on the ship. The ship had open-heart machines and one of the only two hyperbaric chambers in the country. However, because the boat was in constant motion, the staff had to take precautions to secure the beds and medical equipment. Everything, even bottles, had to be tied down.

Murphy worked on the international ward. Most of her patients were Vietnamese women and children. Confined to the ship, she spent her free time playing with the wounded children. It was emotionally difficult to nurse the children back to health and then send them back to face an uncertain future. She and her colleagues had little say about what happened to their patients. Still, they tried their best to help their patients, even if it meant bending the rules.

Once, a GI brought in a malnourished baby girl that he had found in a garbage can. After the nurses stabilized the girl's condition, they were told that they had to send her to an orphanage. But the nurses couldn't find an orphanage they wanted to send her to. "The officer insisted we discharge her, and so we did," Murphy says. "The same day, we happened to admit a baby boy into the ward; we'd just dressed her up in boy's clothes."[2]

She also worked on the orthopedic and general wards. In the orthopedic ward, many patients suffered the loss of multiple limbs, usually by stepping on land mines or during heavy artillery shelling. On the general ward, patients suffered from various illnesses, including malaria. Sometimes, she nursed a patient on the general ward back to health, only to receive the same patient on the orthopedic ward days later, now missing his legs or arms. She began to feel run-down, both mentally and physically. She no longer believed the Vietnamese were the enemy.

CREDIBILITY GAP

In the late 1960s and early 1970s, public distrust in the government and opposition to the war reached an all-time high. In November 1969, the press reported on the investigations of U.S. military atrocities in My Lai. According to reports, a company of U.S. troops entered a Vietnamese village and raped and executed hundreds of unarmed Vietnamese women, children, and men.

In 1971, classified government documents were leaked to the *New York Times*. Known as the Pentagon Papers, the documents revealed that the Gulf of Tonkin Resolution had been drafted months before the incident had allegedly taken place. Although the U.S. government took the *New York Times* to court, claiming that the paper had no right to publish the leaked information, the Supreme Court ruled in favor of the *Times*, citing the protected constitutional right to freedom of the press.

Like others, she questioned the U.S. government's honesty: "The government would report one thing and we'd see something very different.

They would say that we were winning the war and suffering very few casualties, and we'd be inundated with casualties."[3]

When she returned to the United States, Murphy was not sure what she should do. She decided to remain in the military and was assigned to work at a small naval hospital in California. It was difficult to adapt to her new working environment. "I was used to doing really good nursing," she says. "In Vietnam, we were starting IVs, doing major medical dressing changes, writing medical orders—things we were told in nursing school that we would never do."[4] Protocol did not allow her to practice her medical expertise, and so she decided to return to Vietnam. Knowing that there was demand for flight nurses, she signed up for the Air Force Nurse Corps. However, shortly before she was to begin her assignment, Murphy injured her knee and was disqualified from flight status. Eight months later, she left the military for good.

After her experience at the naval hospital, she had little interest in returning to nursing. "At that time, nurses were basically doctors' handmaids," she explains. Instead, she joined a Catholic convent and tried to put her experiences in Vietnam behind her. "I think I was trying to make life

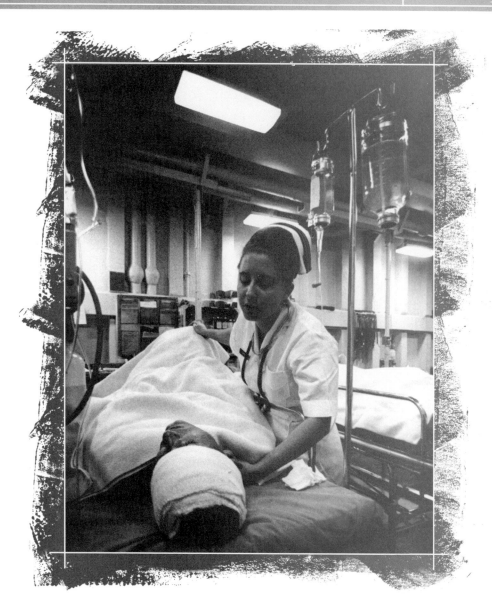

A nurse aboard the USS *Repose* tends to a wounded American soldier. Nurses take care of the many small details of health care—such as the patient's basic physical comfort—that doctors cannot.

saner, because life was pretty confusing to me when I came back," she says. "How do you make sense of a year of being where people were getting killed and maimed? I went looking for some sense and order in the world."[5] She also hoped to recapture the sense of community and purpose she had had in Vietnam.

Murphy didn't find what she was looking for at the convent. She spent the next twenty years living, working, and studying in places across the country. Eventually, after being ordained a minister in the Anglican Church, she moved to Canada where she worked for several years as a parish priest. Currently, she teaches at a seminary.

When the Vietnam Women's Memorial was dedicated, Murphy was asked to volunteer her services as a minister. "It was the first time I'd ever really thought about my time in Vietnam," she says. "Once I started doing that, all hell broke loose."[6] She began to experience severe bouts of depression, anxiety attacks, and flashbacks. At the memorial, she attended a conference on PTSD and recognized that she, too, suffered from the illness. Although PTSD still affects her life, she is able to manage its symptoms with medication and self-awareness. Although fewer Vietnam vets live in Canada, online forums and support groups have put her in contact with other women who served in Vietnam. "Sometimes I just want to forget everything, but it is helpful to know that there are people out there who I can write to and talk to, people who will understand if I'm having a rough time. Unless you've been in a war situation, it's really hard to explain it to somebody,"[7] she says.

Over the past two years, she has returned to Vietnam and plans to continue her visits. "It's been very healing to see what the country is like without war," she says. "You'd think that they would really hate Westerners, but the people are wonderful. They say the war's over, you're our friends, and we're glad you came to see us."[8]

SUSAN O'NEILL, ARMY NURSE CORPS (VIETNAM, 1969–1970)

5

Susan O'Neill was seventeen when she graduated from high school in Fort Wayne, Indiana. She wanted to go to college, but her parents would not sign the loan papers she would need to pay for her education unless she attended a trade school. She decided to go to nursing school, which would provide her with job opportunities.

Then a friend at nursing school in Anderson, Indiana, was going to Chicago to enlist in the army. She asked O'Neill to take a ride to Chicago with her. O'Neill had no

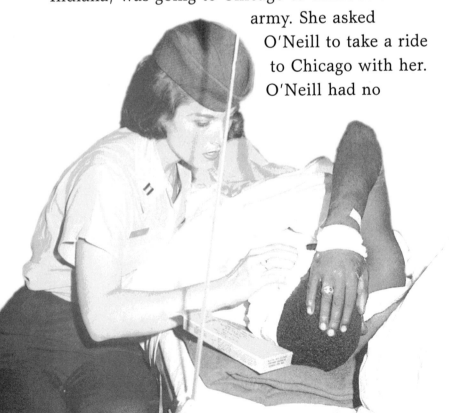

interest in signing up herself—she was part of
the antiwar movement, singing protest songs in
coffeehouses and campaigning for antiwar politi-
cians. Still, she welcomed the chance to leave
town for the weekend.

In Chicago, a recruiter approached O'Neill,
who told her that if she joined the military, the
government would pay for her last year of nursing
school. O'Neill liked the idea of paying back her
parents for her education. Still, she wasn't willing
to go to Vietnam. The recruiter assured her that
she wouldn't: "He said, 'You don't have to worry
about Vietnam, there's a waiting list a mile long
for nurses to go there.'"[1] He told her there was a
good chance that she would be sent to Japan,
Germany, or even Hawaii. O'Neill hadn't had
many opportunities to travel; she decided the offer
was too good to pass up. As she signed the necessary forms that summer of 1967, she thought
about how surprised her friends would be that
she, an antiwar protester, had enlisted.

The military exercises at basic training at
Fort Sam Houston, in Texas, seemed like a waste
of time to O'Neill. Why did she need to learn
how to march or read a compass? Then, during
one orientation, she remembers that an officer

told the trainees, "You might have heard that
there was a waiting list a mile long for nurses to
go to Vietnam. Well, that's no longer true. By
the end of this year, half of you will be there
and the other half will be on orders."[2] O'Neill
was stunned. In May 1969, she had orders to go
to Vietnam.

The flight to Vietnam was long and quiet.
Although the plane was full of servicemen and
-women, few wanted to discuss the war. "We
avoided discussing it; it was a given,"[3] she explains.

O'Neill was assigned to work at the 22nd
Surgical MUST unit (mobile hospital) in Phu Bai,
located in the hills between the demilitarized
zone and Da Nang. Constructed of inflated rubber hung over metal frames, MUST units could
be taken apart quickly and moved as needed.
When she arrived in Phu Bai, O'Neill noticed
that the countryside was covered with mounds of
earth decorated with piles of white stones. Later,
she learned that the U.S. compound had been
built over a Buddhist cemetery. "The tent for the
motor pool actually dissected a grave," she
remembers. "I was outraged. I thought what
would we do if somebody set up in one of
our graveyards?"[4]

Shortly after her arrival, she witnessed her first operating room death. After this initiation, she felt her work in Vietnam had truly begun. Because patients required medical attention on several injuries at once, nurses were asked to perform procedures that they were not normally expected—or even permitted—to do. Among other things, nurses started IVs, picked shrapnel

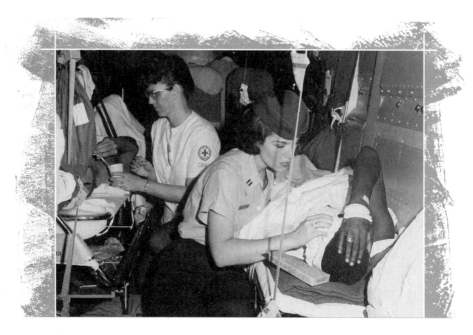

A nurse consoles a soldier who is being transported back to the United States. Many soldiers were so badly wounded that a quick recovery was not likely. In such cases, the soldiers were discharged from military service and were allowed to return home.

SEXUAL HARASSMENT AND RAPE

Women in Vietnam were subject to various forms of sexual harassment and rape. Because the crimes were rarely reported, it is difficult to find statistics on these incidents. One reason for this is because at that time the military—mirroring society at large—did not take such crimes seriously. Often, women themselves were blamed for having provoked the attacks. Some women worried that reporting a colleague or superior might brand them as troublemakers and do harm to their careers. Some feared that admitting that they had been the victim of a sexual assault would demonstrate that they were unable to protect themselves and therefore weaker than their male counterparts. For these and other reasons, sexual harassment has continued to be a problem in the military.

---

out of wounds, cut away dead tissue, and clipped damaged blood vessels.

On the rare occasions that she had free time, O'Neill socialized with the enlisted men who worked around her. The experience of

being a woman amid hundreds of men was
strange. "People looked at you symbolically
more than anything," she explains. "You were
the woman they couldn't have, because sheer
numbers said they couldn't. You were pressured
for a lot of things. There were a number of
women who I've talked to who were raped over
there. I was very lucky. There was an attempt;
luckily, I managed to foil it."[5]

By July 1969, the United States was beginning
its plan to "Vietnamize" the war—that is, turn over
the responsibility of fighting the North Vietnamese
army to the South Vietnamese government. The
numbers of U.S. troops stationed in Vietnam were
scaled back. Two months after O'Neill's arrival in
Phu Bai, the MUST unit was packed up and its
staff dispersed to other hospitals. O'Neill was sent
to work at the 27th Surgical at Chu Lai. The hospital was one of two on a sprawling military
complex, situated south of Phu Bai, on the coast of
South China Sea.

The small, overworked staff at the 22nd MUST
unit in Phu Bai had had little time to follow the
demands of military protocol. The hospital at Chu
Lai, however, was far less busy. Also, a number of
"lifers," or people intending to make a career out of

"VIETNAMIZING" THE WAR

"We Americans are a do-it-yourself people. We are an impatient people. Instead of teaching someone else to do a job, we like to do it ourselves. And this trait has been carried over into our foreign policy. In the previous administration, we Americanized the war in Vietnam. In this administration, we are Vietnamizing the search for peace . . . Under the new orders, the primary mission of our troops is to enable the South Vietnamese forces to assume the full responsibility for the security of South Vietnam . . . We have adopted a plan which we have worked out in cooperation with the South Vietnamese for the complete withdrawal of all U.S. combat ground forces, and their replacement by South Vietnamese forces . . . It is not the easy way. It is the right way."[6]

—President Richard Nixon,
Address to the Nation, November 3, 1969

---

their military service, were based in Chu Lai. The hospital was far more concerned about proper military conduct. Dress codes, obligatory saluting, and

rules of fraternization—officers were not allowed to
socialize with enlisted men or women—were
strictly enforced. O'Neill didn't care for such rules.
She was often in trouble with the hospital's head
nurse. O'Neill requested a transfer. The head nurse
told her she would transfer her into one of the
heaviest combat zones in Vietnam—the 12th
Evacuation Hospital in Cu Chi.

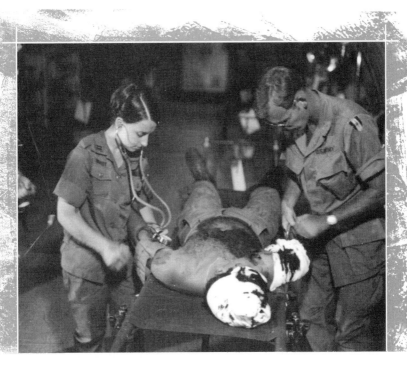

Army nurses Captain Bernice Scott and Lieutenant David Van Voohris
cut the field bandages from a newly arrived patient, 2nd Surgical
Hospital, Lai Khe, Vietnam, September 1969.

Although the assignment was supposed to be a punishment, O'Neill was glad to be in Cu Chi. "I wanted to go some place that was relatively busy," she says. "You have to think too much if you have a lot of spare time. I was asking myself entirely too many questions and getting pretty depressed. 'Why am I here? What good am I doing? If I'm opposed to this war, am I morally bound to leave?'"[7] As long as she was busy helping patients, she felt useful and could justify being in Vietnam.

O'Neill counted the days until her return to the United States. At the same time, she wondered how she would fit in. She had kept in touch with her family by trading recorded tapes, but she rarely talked about the war. She didn't want them to worry. Once, though, toward the end of her assignment, she sat outside when she was making her tape, so the sounds of artillery shelling could be heard. "I wanted them to think in terms of the war, because they believed most anything the government said. I was pretty bitter at that point. I wanted them to get the atmosphere of it and realize that there was something going on over here,"[8] she remembers.

Twenty-four hours after O'Neill left Vietnam, she arrived at a military base in Oakland, California.

She remembers walking down a long corridor that seemed to go on forever. "At the end of it, there was a mural of a soldier standing there with a flag," she says. "Underneath was written, 'Welcome Back Soldier—Your Country is Proud of You.'" O'Neill knew this wasn't true. Most Americans were not proud of Vietnam vets; many were ashamed. They felt that vets had killed innocent civilians and destroyed villages for no reason. "We followed the news," she said. "You could get the *New York Times* and *Time* magazine, so you knew what was going on."[9]

Rather than return to Indiana, O'Neill decided to stay in Oakland. There she met with a boyfriend, the hospital registrar with whom she had worked in Cu Chi. He asked her to marry him, and O'Neill accepted. Because she had a companion who understood and shared so many of her experiences in Vietnam, O'Neill believes that the relationship saved her from experiencing some of the psychological problems that other, more isolated vets, faced.

Twenty-five years after O'Neill returned from Vietnam, she began writing about her experiences in Vietnam. Ballantine Books published a collection of these stories, *Don't Mean Nothing*, in 2001. In her introduction to the collection, O'Neill writes: "I joined the army for the money and the travel, and because I was naive and had no idea what I would be getting myself into. It was one of the biggest learning experiences of my life."[10]

DIANA SEBEK
ARMY NURSE CORPS
(VIETNAM, 1970)

6

When Diana Sebek was a young girl growing up in Chicago, she fell in love with the glorified images of World War II nurses and nuns she had seen in books and movies. "There was a John Wayne movie showing nuns walking into battle to deliver care to the wounded soldiers," she recalls. "They just walked right through the gunfire and were so powerful, they weren't hurt. In my six-year-old mind, I thought that was marvelous."[1]

Sebek also saw as a role model an aunt who was a nurse. Sebek admired the pictures of

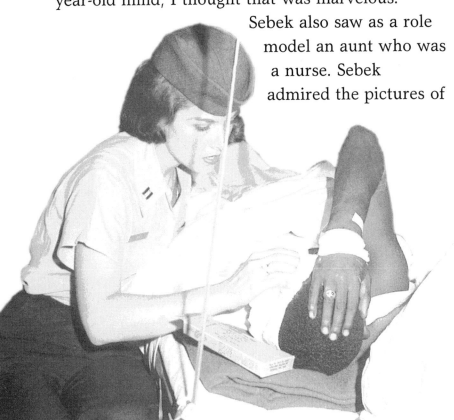

Navy nurses receive Purple Heart medals for injuries received in the Christmas Eve 1964 bombing of Brink Bachelor Officers Quarters, Republic of Vietnam. Despite being noncombatants, nurses were so close to the front lines that injuries and deaths occurred throughout the war.

her aunt dressed in her starched white nursing cap and uniform. Being a nurse seemed both noble and adventuresome. With these images in mind, Sebek enrolled at a local nursing school program at the South Chicago Community Hospital after graduating from high school.

While Sebek was a nursing student, nine of her fellow classmates were brutally raped and murdered in their dormitory by a drifter named

Richard Speck. Now, more than thirty-five years later, Sebek says that the tragic event may have prompted her decision to enlist in the military; perhaps she was seeking greater security. A roommate who was already enlisted introduced Sebek to the army student-nursing program. When army recruiters offered to pay one year of tuition in exchange for two years of active military service, Sebek joined without a second thought.

Busy in nursing school, she was sheltered from news about the war. On the rare occasions when Sebek had free time, watching television was the last thing she wanted to do. Consequently, she had little idea what she might be facing. "The thought of going to war was not even in my head," she says. "Basically, I thought I could pay my parents back for school. And then when I was in the service, I wouldn't have to worry about a place to live; it was kind of like marrying Uncle Sam."[2]

After Sebek graduated and passed her state board exams, she was officially on duty. Her first requirement was to report to Fort Sam Houston for basic training. She sat in an auditorium with other nurses and doctors, where they learned about military insignia and protocol or, as she puts it, "who you were expected to salute, who was expected to salute you."[3] She also learned to march in formation. "I hated marching," she says. "It was like being in a meat market, like cattle being moved around. The guys on the side would whistle and make noises."[4] More useful was the additional medical combat training, including learning how to perform tracheotomies (making air passages in the throat by cutting a hole in the trachea).

At the time of her training, Sebek was engaged to an antiwar activist. He wanted to get her pregnant in order to release her from her military service. But during basic training, Sebek felt herself beginning to change. She realized there were more opportunities open to her other than marriage and motherhood. She broke up with her fiancé. "And then the world was in front of me," she remembers. "I was joining the army, not thinking or worrying about war or people getting killed."[5]

On December 5, 1969, Sebek was at the airport, waiting to fly to Vietnam. Her family all came to see her off. During the picture taking and farewells, she was scared, but excited: "I was the man in the 1962 movie *Hemingway's Adventures of a Young Man*," she recalls. "I was a young woman, but I was going to have the same adventures as a man."[6]

The twenty-four-hour flight to Vietnam was long and tiring. Aside from the flight attendants, Sebek was the only female aboard the plane. Not that this bothered her: "I talked to the guys. To me, there was no difference between me and them. We were army; we were going over, fine. It's amazing how naive I was."[7]

She landed at an airport in Cam Rahn Bay, where she was struck by the smell of burning garbage and bodies. Here she had to wait for another flight to take her up north to her destination, Quang Tri, to a hospital close to the demilitarized zone. It was a marine hospital connected to a Vietnamese children's hospital. Many of the wounded were army and air force service men and Vietnamese children caught in the crossfire of battle. Originally assigned to work in an operating room, Sebek worked where she was most needed—in triage.

In triage, nurses and corpsmen (military field medics) separated the wounded according to who needed to be seen by the surgeon first. Soldiers with less severe injuries were set aside. Sometimes, if a soldier was likely to die, the medical staff had to move on to treat those men who had a chance of living. Determining which patients would die and which might live was traumatic. Many triage nurses were burdened by guilt and questioned their decisions for the rest of their lives.

It is extremely difficult for Sebek to talk about what she saw and did that year. Every day, she was faced with critically wounded and dying men. She cleaned their wounds and sent them to the operating room where they were put under anesthesia. She never got a chance to talk to them or connect their faces with names. Some of the friends she made in Vietnam were killed. She became severely depressed and had trouble coming to terms with what she was seeing and doing in Vietnam. A doctor prescribed antidepressants and sent her to a hospital in Da Nang to see a psychiatrist.

As it turns out, the psychiatrist Sebek was assigned to see was not working *at* the hospital, but was a patient *in* the hospital. While she waited for him to see her, she saw the movie *M*A*S*H*, a dark comedy about U.S. military doctors and nurses in the Korean War. The movie helped Sebek realize that her depression and feelings of futility over the war were normal. "It gave some validation to the fact that the war was a farce,"[8] she says. When she heard that her unit was receiving mass casualties, she returned to work without having seen the psychiatrist.

When her tour of duty was over, Sebek was ready to go home. The return was more difficult than she had imagined. "I did not realize that people were calling Vietnam veterans 'baby-killers,' that there were actually people who hated us."[9] When she told people that she had served in

Above, actress Dana Delaney (*second from left*) in a scene from *China Beach*, a television series about nurses, soldiers, volunteers, and entertainers serving in Vietnam. The series aired from 1988 to 1991 and took an uncompromising look at the effect the war had on both Americans and the Vietnamese.

"BABY-KILLERS"

In March 1968, a company of U.S. troops advanced on the village of My Lai and proceeded to systematically rape and murder hundreds of unarmed, Vietnamese civilians. Once these actions were exposed, the American public was outraged. Some expressed their anger both physically and verbally at Vietnam vets. Many believed that the massacre was not an isolated incident:

> Although it may be that the My Lai massacre is an "isolated incident," in the sense that no other report of mass killing of civilians . . . has been brought to light, there can be no doubt that such an atrocity was possible only because . . . killing civilians and destroying their villages had come to be the rule, and not the exception, in our conduct of war. And the scale of this killing and destruction had been great enough . . . to defeat completely our original purpose in going into Vietnam, which was to save the South Vietnamese people from coercion by the enemy.[10]

> —*"Notes and Comment,"* New Yorker, *December 20, 1969*

Vietnam, people turned away from her. "It was personal," she says. "I thought I was unlovable. I thought it was Diana, not the fact that I was a Vietnam veteran."[11]

She began to suffer from post-traumatic stress disorder. She found it impossible to talk to anyone and wanted to be alone. Her family reacted to her growing isolation with anger and confusion: "My mother told me that the army 'messed' me up, only that wasn't the word she used. I had to move out of the house because I couldn't handle being told that I was so 'messed' up."[12]

She took a job at a veterans hospital. Because the patients had been in wars themselves, Sebek felt accepted. She tried to contact a few of the people she'd known in Vietnam, but survivor's guilt eventually made her afraid to keep in touch. Were her friends still alive? Would they be missing a leg or arm? Rather than risk learning more tragic news, she avoided her past experiences as much as possible.

Over the next thirty years, Sebek struggled with PTSD. Recently, she began experiencing severe flashbacks at work and was forced to retire. Currently she is in therapy, trying to cope with the symptoms of PTSD. Part of her therapy is to remember and talk about what she experienced in

Vietnam. The memories create physical and emotional pain. "People were sent to just kill," she says. "It was disgusting, animal against animal. I have so many empty spaces in my head about things that occurred there. I don't know what memories are there. Going back is hard."[13]

WOMEN IN THE LINE OF FIRE

7

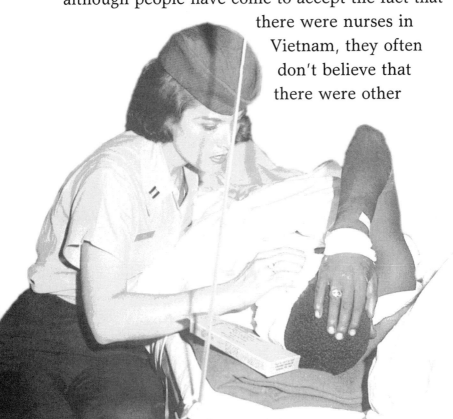

Over the past twenty years, public awareness about women serving in Vietnam has increased. Much of this awareness is due to the fact that the women themselves have begun talking about their experiences. Even so, some people are not open to the idea. Marilyn Roth, a member of the Women's Army Corps who wrote encoded messages for helicopter pilots in Vietnam in 1968, says that although people have come to accept the fact that there were nurses in Vietnam, they often don't believe that there were other

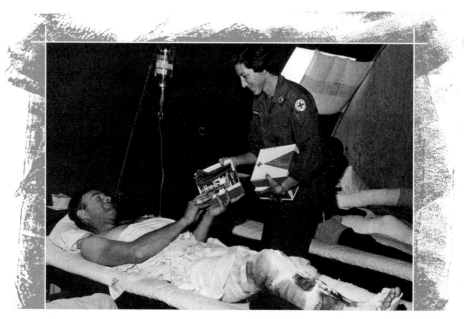

His leg nearly severed from a mine explosion, Sergeant William Mullen rehabilitates at the 85th Evacuation Hospital in Qui Nhon, South Vietnam. Cheered by a civilian volunteer's smiles and attentive care, Mullen accepts a Red Cross comfort kit.

women there as well: "As an enlisted woman in Vietnam, very few people know or understand what we were doing there. I have a license plate on my car that says 'Served in Vietnam,' and I get stopped lots of times at a red light when the windows are down and a guy would say, 'Oh, where were you stationed? Were you a nurse?' And I would say, 'I was enlisted,' and they wouldn't even talk to me. They would just take right off."[1]

In addition to those enlisted in the military, thousands of civilian women volunteered to go to Vietnam to support the troops, the U.S. government, and the Vietnamese civilian population. Some were foreign service employees and worked for the CIA, the U.S. Embassy, and with USAID. Others were part of the military civilian workforce, working for the Armed Forces Radio and Television, the Military Assistance Command Vietnam, or the Army Special Services.

The Red Cross Supplemental Recreational Activities Overseas program sent women ages twenty-one to twenty-five to Vietnam to boost the morale of American troops. Nicknamed "donut dollies," the women ran recreation centers throughout Vietnam. They also went out to remote areas in the mountains and jungles to entertain the troops. Because the roads were dangerous, they were usually transported by helicopter. They invented their own programs, lugging canvas bags filled with homemade games and prizes out with them to the fields. Although the games were silly, most men welcomed the distraction and the company.

The United Service Organization (USO), founded by various religious groups, also ran recreation clubs for soldiers. The USO recruited

Janet Small (left) walks away from the helicopter that just dropped her off along with Eileen Conoboy and Linda Morgan. These three women worked for the Red Cross "Donut Dollies" at Quan Loi in 1967. Donut Dollies ran recreation centers for the troops, and entertained troops in remote areas.

women to work as hostesses at the centers, where soldiers could eat, play cards and Ping-Pong, get free haircuts, make overseas calls, or see a concert. At the USO center in Tan Son Nhut, volunteer Maureen Nerli recalls, "We served between five hundred and eight hundred shakes, hot dogs, and hamburgers every day."[2]

Other organizations focused on aiding Vietnamese civilians. The American Friends Service Committee, a Quaker organization, worked to bring medical assistance to war victims. In the

Peace Corps and the International Volunteer Service, women helped build schools, run health clinics and orphanages, and provide other humanitarian assistance.

Women reporters and photographers went to Vietnam to cover the war. Most worked freelance, without the security or benefit of working for a newspaper or television network. Dickey Chapelle, an experienced war photographer who contributed to *Life, Reader's Digest,* and *National Geographic,* began covering the war in Vietnam in 1961. She died on November 4, 1965, when a land mine exploded while she was on patrol with a group of marines. Marguerite Higgins, a journalist who contributed to *Newsday* and the *New York Herald Tribune,* made

Dickey Chapelle mounts a camera and readies herself for action at the Don Phuc command post on the Vietnam-Cambodia frontier. Chapelle stayed at this compound for more than a month, taking pictures and interviewing combatants.

COVERING THE WAR

In *Inside Television's First War*, NBC's Saigon bureau chief Ron Steinman writes about prevailing attitudes toward women correspondents:

> When I ran the bureau, I helped—with the agreement of the New York management—to keep women correspondents out of Vietnam. The prohibition of women reporters became an unwritten rule throughout my stay; in the 1960s they were a small minority in broadcasting and had a long way to go before gaining acceptance . . . A woman covering combat? No thanks. I worried about facilities in the field. Bathrooms? Showers? Where would she sleep? Would she have enough strength to troop through the jungle? . . . Though women had covered other wars, and covered them with distinction, I did not believe a woman television reporter belonged in Vietnam covering this war. I make no excuses for my behavior. I was a man of my time, not a pioneer.[3]

several trips to Vietnam, beginning in 1963. On her tenth trip to Vietnam in 1965, she contracted a tropical disease and passed away shortly afterward. Other notable female journalists include *New York Times* correspondent Gloria Emerson, who won the George Polk Award for Excellence in Foreign Reporting in 1971, and war correspondent Martha Gellhorn, whose reports were so graphic they were sometimes rejected by her editors.

Although women were not officially allowed to serve on the front lines of combat zones in Vietnam, they often did. Combat zones are often defined by politics rather than actual battle lines. For instance, during the early years of the Vietnam War, men were denied combat pay and compensation because the U.S. government did not want to admit to the public that the military was engaged in combat. Similarly, because few wanted to acknowledge that women were in the line of fire, actual combat zones were not always designated as such. Sometimes, the same location was designated a noncombat zone for women and a combat zone for men.

No matter what their job titles, most women who served in Vietnam suffered trauma. They witnessed death, destruction, and maiming. Because they were women, they were expected to provide comfort and cheer even when they themselves felt none. They held men's hands as they were dying and became surrogate mothers, wives, and girlfriends to men whose loved ones were far away. They tended the needs of others, with little time or energy left over to care for themselves.

Patience Mason, who has written and spoken extensively on the effects of PTSD on Vietnam veterans and their families, says that it only occurred to her recently that civilian women suffered from PTSD. "I had no idea that donut dollies in their little blue uniforms, playing games with the men, had traumatic experiences," she says. "It shows how ignorant you can be; they were right there in the middle of everything with everybody else. Somehow because they weren't in the army or military, it never occurred to me that they were in danger."[4]

Today, women have a much more integrated presence in the military. According to an profile in the *New York Times Magazine* in February 2003, 15 percent of all active-duty military personnel are women. Although women are banned from frontline battle and have not broken into assignments that demand certain physical requirements, they work in more than 90 percent of all military fields.

Although many women in Vietnam (and in other wars) put themselves in the line of fire, the

PHYSIOLOGICAL DIFFERENCES

The army's *Physical Training Manual* lists physical differences between men and women as the basis of lower physical training requirements for women, including:

- The average eighteen-year-old man is 70.2 inches tall and weighs 144.8 pounds; the average eighteen-year-old woman is 64.6 inches tall and weighs 126.6 pounds.

- Men have 50 percent greater total muscle mass, based on weight, than women.

- A woman who is the same size as her male counterpart generally is only 80 percent as strong. Therefore, men usually have advantage in strength, speed, and power over women.

- Women become fatigued faster than men because their heart rates are five to eight beats per minute faster.

- Women respond to heat stress differently from men. Women sweat less, lose less heat through evaporation, and reach higher body temperatures before sweating starts.[5]

—*Field Manual 21-20: Physical Readiness Training*, Department of the Army, 1992 idea of women in combat remains controversial. Marie de Young, a captain in the U.S. Reserves, argues that women lack the emotional and physical requirements to engage in combat: "We would never send an undertrained welterweight boxer into a ring with a world champion heavyweight boxer . . . Until women are willing to give up the privilege of stereotyped but legally defined lower standards of physical fitness, performance, and personal conduct, they should be excluded from the heavyweight ring, and the ground combat exclusion policy should be retained."[6]

Others feel that women are as capable of engaging in combat as men. Colonel Lorry M. Fenner, a vice wing commander in the air force's 70th Intelligence Wing, notes that women don't have a problem fighting. Instead, Colonel Fenner feels society has a problem allowing women to serve in combat roles: "The idea that American society will not tolerate—and American fighting men cannot endure—harm to women is simply inconsistent with the realities of most wars; enemy and even allied civilian women are routinely killed or harmed. The inclusion of female military causalities in our reckoning, however, dilutes the effectiveness of the 'killing women and children' propaganda. It brings all too close to the surface the possibility that we do not object to killing women in war but to women killing."[7]

Like their male counterparts, women who served in Vietnam faced unimaginable physical and mental circumstances. Likewise, when they returned home, they found that few wanted to hear about their experiences. Isolated from society and even from one another, their questions about the war stood unresolved. What had they accomplished

Since the Vietnam War, women have played a more and more visible role in the United States military. Today there are approximately 200,000 women serving in the United States armed forces. Currently, most of these women serve in the army and the air force.

in Vietnam? How could they rationalize the brutality and destruction that had surrounded them?

Over the past thirty years, female Vietnam veterans have struggled to come to terms with these questions. Although their experiences were traumatic, many women feel that the war ultimately gave them better perspective on nationalism, religion, war, and humanity. Many stress the importance of serving one's country and fellow humans, as well as closely observing and being critical of one's government. They believe that these two responsibilities are not and should not be mutually exclusive. They understand, perhaps better than anyone, the consequences of war. Time will tell how these women's service and continued contributions will influence the politics of war.

TIMELINE

939 Chinese driven out of Vietnam. Era of Vietnamese independence begins.

1858–1873 French attack cities throughout Vietnam.

1884 French colonial era begins.

1930 Ho Chi Minh establishes Indochinese Communist Party and organizes campaign to win Vietnamese independence.

1940 Japan places Vietnam under military occupation. Local French authority is weakened to figurehead status.

1945 Japanese surrender to the Allies. Vietnamese Communist Party under Ho Chi Minh declares Vietnam's independence as the Democratic Republic of Vietnam (DRV). French troops return to Vietnam.

1950 United States begins policy to give economic and military aid to French troops in Vietnam.

1954 French troops are defeated. Geneva Accords divide Vietnam at the 17th Parallel. North Vietnam is independent under a Socialist government. South Vietnam is governed as a republic under President Ngo Dinh Diem, with U.S. support. Elections to unite two regions under one government are to be held in two years.

1955 President Diem announces elections won't take place. United States begins sending money and military advisers to South Vietnam.

1956 Vietnamese Communists push President Diem for elections. Diem cracks down on political opponents.

TIMELINE Cont.

1959 North Vietnam sends weapons and supplies to the Vietcong on the Ho Chi Minh Trail.

1960 Newly elected U.S. president John F. Kennedy promises to help South Vietnam.

1963 President Diem killed in military coup. More than 16,300 U.S. military personnel stationed in Vietnam.

1964 Lyndon B. Johnson is elected president. U.S. Congress passes Gulf of Tonkin Resolution, giving President Johnson authority to take military action against North Vietnam in response to an alleged North Vietnamese attack on the USS *Maddox*, a U.S. Navy destroyer that had been in the gulf, spying on North Vietnam. During his presidency, Johnson uses the resolution to justify sending increasing numbers of troops to fight in Vietnam.

1965 First combat troops, army and navy nurses, and civilian volunteers arrive in Vietnam.

1967 President Johnson allows women to achieve general and admiral rank.

1968 Tet Offensive by North Vietnamese army and its sympathizers is waged against targets in South Vietnam on January 31. Richard M. Nixon is elected U.S. president.

1969 Ho Chi Minh dies on September 3. United States begins plan to "Vietnamize" the war. More than 60,000 American soldiers are withdrawn from Vietnam.

1970 United States and North Vietnam begin secret negotiations to end war. U.S. National Guard opens fire on students during antiwar rally at Kent State University, killing four students and injuring nine others.

1971 *New York Times* publishes the Pentagon Papers, classified government documents leaked to the press indicating that the U.S. government had been intentionally dishonest to the public about its involvement in Vietnam.

1972 On March 29, the last contingent of American nurses leaves Vietnam. More than 5,000 nurses served during the war; the average age was 23.6 years old.

August 11, 1972 Last U.S. combat troops withdraw from Vietnam. Nixon is reelected

1973 The United States and North Vietnam sign a cease-fire agreement in Paris on January 27. U.S. ground troops withdraw from Vietnam.

1975 The South Vietnamese army retreats under a North Vietnamese offensive. The last Americans are evacuated on April 29. North Vietnamese troops enter Saigon on April 30. Congress orders three military academies to accept women cadets.

1976 North and South Vietnam are united as the Socialist Republic of Vietnam.

1977 Socialist Republic of Vietnam is admitted to United Nations.

1982 Vietnam Veterans Memorial is dedicated in Washington, D.C., on November 11.

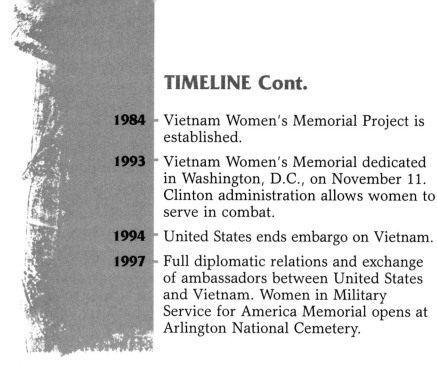

TIMELINE Cont.

1984 — Vietnam Women's Memorial Project is established.

1993 — Vietnam Women's Memorial dedicated in Washington, D.C., on November 11. Clinton administration allows women to serve in combat.

1994 — United States ends embargo on Vietnam.

1997 — Full diplomatic relations and exchange of ambassadors between United States and Vietnam. Women in Military Service for America Memorial opens at Arlington National Cemetery.

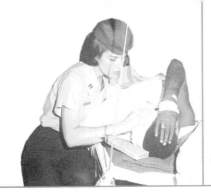

Glossary

Communist One in favor of establishing a Communist political system, similar to the Communist Party system established in Russia in 1917. In theory, under Communism, society's economic and social needs are determined and met by the state, rather than by a free-market economy or social class.

DMZ Acronym for "demilitarized zone." The area surrounding the 17th Parallel division between North and South Vietnam where some of the heaviest fighting took place during the Vietnam War.

fraternization Association with others in a friendly, brotherly way, usually in violation of rules or orders that prohibit such interactions.

GI Term to refer to an ordinary "government issue" soldier.

Hippocratic oath An oath of ethical and moral conduct sworn by those in the medical profession, particularly doctors and nurses; attributed to the Greek physician Hippocrates (460–377 BC), known as the father of science.

Ho Chi Minh (1890–1969) Greatly admired Vietnamese Communist leader who led the struggle to liberate Vietnam from foreign rule;

when Vietnam was divided, he became the leader of North Vietnam's Democratic Republic of Vietnam.

Ho Chi Minh Trail A maze of footpaths and roads used by the North Vietnamese army and Vietcong soldiers to ship supplies from North Vietnam to South Vietnam.

hooch A general term for hutlike living quarters used to house military personnel in base camps; also used to refer to the thatch and bamboo homes of the rural Vietnamese.

medevac Medical evacuation, or transporting a patient from one location to another for medical reasons.

MUST Acronym for medical unit self-transportable. A hospital constructed in such a way that it can be moved easily from one area to another.

North Vietnam As part of the 1954 negotiations for France's withdrawal from Vietnam, France and North Vietnam agreed to divide Vietnam at the 17th Parallel, between the predominately Communist northern part of the country and the retreating French and their Vietnamese supporters in the southern part.

post-traumatic stress disorder (PTSD) A psychological disorder caused by witnessing an extremely traumatic event; symptoms include flashbacks, amnesia, depression, and uncontrollable emotional and physical reactions to stimuli.

prisoner of war (POW) A soldier who has been captured by the opposing military forces.

South Vietnam After Vietnam was divided at the 17th Parallel, South Vietnam was ruled by President Ngo Dinh Diem. In order to keep South Vietnam from a North Vietnamese Communist takeover, U.S. president Johnson approved a U.S. military offensive against North Vietnam.

Supplemental Recreational Activities Overseas (SRAO) A Red Cross program designed to boost the morale of U.S. troops.

Tet Offensive A major military campaign against cities and towns throughout South Vietnam led by the Communist forces in North and South Vietnam.

tracheotomy A surgical operation in which an opening is cut into the throat and windpipe, or trachea, in order to create an alternative passage for breathing when the regular airway passage is blocked.

Vietcong (VC) Refers to Vietnamese Communists and their supporters who fought against South Vietnamese and U.S. troops during the Vietnam War; taken from the Vietnamese equivalent for "Vietnamese Communist," *Viet-nam Cong-san.*

Vietnam Veterans Memorial Commonly referred to as the Wall, the Washington, D.C., memorial is a black, granite wall built in 1982 and dedicated to U.S. servicemen and -women who died or went missing during their tours of duty in Vietnam. The polished stone is carved with more than 58,000 names. In 1993, the Vietnam Women's Memorial, a sculpture depicting three nurses tending to a wounded soldier, was added to honor women who served in the war.

Women's Army Corps (WAC) An auxiliary noncombat army unit established for women volunteers by the U.S. Congress in 1942. By the end of World War II, more than 99,000 women had served in the WAC, both overseas and in the United States. In 1948, Congress passed the Women's Armed Services Integration Act, and the WAC became part of the regular army.

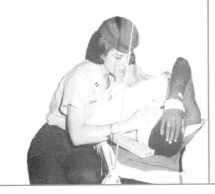

For More Information

Canadian Nurses Foundation
50 Driveway
Ottawa, ON K2P 1E2
Canada
(613) 237-2159
e-mail: info@cnursesfdn.ca
Web site: http://www.canadiannursesfoundation.com

Canadian Vietnam Veterans
    Association—Edmonton
14212-106 Avenue
Edmonton, AB T5N 1B4
Canada
(403) 454-2710

National Vietnam Veterans Coalition
100 Connecticut Avenue NW Suite 1200
Washington, DC 20036

Sharon Ann Lane Foundation
P.O. Box 90
Media, PA 19063
(610) 892-4964
e-mail: mach06@earthlink.net
Web site: http://www.sharonannlanefoundation.org

Veterans of Foreign Wars of the United States
National Headquarters
406 West 34th Street
Kansas City, MO 64111
(816) 756-3390
e-mail: info@vfw.org
Web site: http://www.vfw.org

Vietnam Veterans Against the War
National Office
P.O. Box 408594
Chicago, IL 60640
(773) 327-5756
e-mail: vvaw@prairienet.org
Web site: http://www.vvaw.org

Vietnam Women's Memorial Foundation
1735 Connecticut Avenue NW, 3rd Floor
Washington, DC 20009
(866) 822-8963
e-mail: vwmfdc@aol.com
Web site: http://www.vietnamwomensmemorial.org

Videocassettes:
The First Vietnam War: 1946–1954; Vietnam: A Television History, Vol. 2. Boston: WGBH, 1983.
A Healing. Connie Stevens. 1997.

Not on the Frontline. Nebraska: EVT, 1991.
The Other Angels. Patricia L. Walsh. Boulder, CO: Other Angels Productions, 1995.
Their Own Vietnam. Nancy Kates. 1995.

WEB SITES

Due to the changing nature of Internet links, the Rosen Publishing Group, Inc., has developed an online list of Web sites related to the subject of this book. This site is updated regularly. Please use this link to access the list:

http://www.rosenlinks.com/aww/viwa

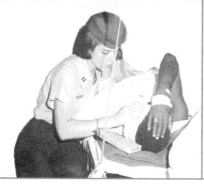

For Further Reading

Denenberg, Barry. *Voices from Vietnam.* New York: Scholastic, 1995.

Freedman, Dan, and Jacqueline Rhoads, eds. *Nurses in Vietnam: The Forgotten Veterans.* Austin: Texas Monthly Press, 1987.

Holm, Major General Jeanne. *Women in the Military: An Unfinished Revolution.* Novato, CA: Presidio Press, 1992.

Marshall, Kathryn. *In the Combat Zone: An Oral History of American Women in Vietnam, 1966–1975.* Boston: Little, Brown & Co., 1987.

Mason, Patience H. C. *Recovering from the War: A Woman's Guide to Helping Your Vietnam Vet, Your Family and Yourself.* New York: Penguin, 1990.

Norman, Elizabeth. *Women at War: The Story of Fifty Military Nurses Who Served in Vietnam.* Philadelphia: University of Pennsylvania Press, 1990.

O'Neill, Susan. *Don't Mean Nothing: Short Stories of Vietnam.* New York: Ballantine Books, 2001.

Shulimson, Jack. *TET—1968.* Toronto: Bantam Books, 1989.

Smith, Winne. *American Daughter Gone to War: On the Front Lines with an Army Nurse in Vietnam.* New York: William Morrow and Company, 1992.

Walker, Keith. *A Piece of My Heart: The Stories of Twenty-six American Women Who Served in Vietnam.* Novato, CA: Presidio Press, 1985.

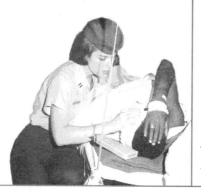

Bibliography

Berthelsen, John. "Bush Should Heed Lessons of Vietnam." *Asia Times*, February 22, 2003. Retrieved March 3, 2003 (http://www.atimes.com/atimes/Southeast_Asia/EB22Ae02.html).

Bigler, Philip. *Hostile Fire: The Life and Death of First Lieutenant Sharon Lane.* Arlington, VA: Vandamere Press, 1996.

Bunn, Austin. "Unarmed and Under Fire: An Oral History of Female Vietnam Vets." Salon.com, November 11, 1999. Retrieved March 3, 2003 (http://www.salon.com/mwt/feature/1999/11/11/women).

Diagnostic and Statistical Manual of Mental Disorders, third edition. Washington, DC: American Psychiatric Association, 1987.

"Dr. Thomas A. Dooley, Biography." Retrieved March 3, 2003 (http://www.umsl.edu/~whmc/exhibits/dooleybio.htm).

Evans, Diane Carlson. "Moving a Vision: The Vietnam Women's Memorial." Retrieved March 3, 2003 (http://www.vietnamwomensmemorial.org/pages/pdf/dcevans.pdf).

Evans, Diane Carlson. Telephone interview. April 17, 2003.

Fennel, Kathy. Telephone interview. April 20, 2003.

Fenner, Lorry M., and Marie E. de Young. *Women in Combat: Civic Duty or Military Liability?* Washington, DC: Georgetown University Press, 2001.

Gruhzit-Hoyt, Olga. *A Time Remembered: American Women in the Vietnam War.* Novato, CA: Presidio Press, 1999.

Koehn, Donna. "Military Museum of Their Own," *Tampa Tribune*, April 4, 2001, p. 1.

Mason, Patience. Telephone interview. April 14, 2003.

Murphy, Beth Marie. Telephone interview. April 18, 2003.

No Time for Tears: Vietnam: The Women Who Served. Videocassette. West End Films, Inc., 1993.

Olson, James, and Rancy Roberts. *Mai Lai: A Brief History with Documents.* Boston: Bedford Books, 1998.

O'Neill, Susan. Telephone interview. April 12, 2003.

"Portfolio: Warrior Women." *New York Times Magazine,* February 16, 2003.

Rozell, Barbara. Telephone interview. April 12, 2003.

Scheider, Pat. "Women Veterans Sought for Benefits" *Capital Times,* November 10, 2001, p. 2.

Sebek, Diana. Telephone interview. April 16, 2003.

Skaine, Rosemarie. *Women at War: Gender Issues of Americans in Combat.* Jefferson, NC: McFarland & Co., 1999.

Steinman, Ron. *Inside Television's First War: A Saigon Journal.* Columbia, MO: University of Missouri Press, 2002.

Templer, Robert. *Shadows and Wind: A View of Modern Vietnam.* New York: Penguin Books, 1999.

Turner, Karen Gottschang, and Phan Thanh Hao. *Even the Women Must Fight: Memories of War from North Vietnam.* New York: John Wiley & Sons, 1998.

Zeinert, Karen. *The Valiant Women of the Vietnam War.* Brookfield, CT: Millbrook Press, 2000.

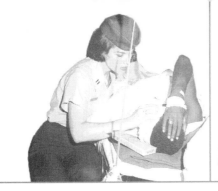

Source Notes

Chapter One
1. Kathy Fennel, telephone interview, April 20, 2003.
2. Ibid.
3. James S. Olson and Randy Roberts, *My Lai: A Brief History with Documents* (Boston: Bedford Books, 1998), pp. 38–41.
4. Fennel.
5. Ibid.
6. Ibid.
7. Ibid.

Chapter Two
1. Barbara Rozell, telephone interview, April 12, 2003.
2. Ibid.
3. Ibid.
4. Ibid.
5. Ibid.
6. Ibid.
7. Ibid.
8. John Berthesel, "Bush Should Heed Lessons of Vietnam," *Asia Times,* February 22, 2003. Retrieved March 3, 2003 (http://www.atimes.com/atimes/Southeast_Asia/EB22AE02.html).
9. Rozell.
10. Ibid.

Chapter Three
1. Diane Carlson Evans, telephone interview, April 20, 2003.
2. Ibid.

3. Ibid.
4. Ibid.
5. Ibid.
6. Ibid.
7. Ibid.
8. Ibid.
9. American Psychiatric Association, *The Diagnostic and Statistical Manual of Mental Disorders,* third edition (Washington, DC: American Psychiatric Association, 1987), pp. 247–251.
10. Diane Carlson Evans, "Moving a Vision: The Vietnam Women's Memorial," retrieved September 12, 2003 (http://www.vietnamwomensmemorial.org/pages/pdf/dcevans.pdf).

Chapter Four

1. Beth Marie Murphy, telephone interview, April 18, 2003.
2. Ibid.
3. Ibid.
4. Ibid.
5. Ibid.
6. Ibid.
7. Ibid.
8. Ibid.

Chapter Five

1. Susan O'Neill, telephone interview, April 12, 2003.
2. Ibid.
3. Ibid.
4. Ibid.
5. Ibid.
6. Richard Nixon, Address to the Nation, November 3, 1969.
7. O'Neill.
8. Ibid.

9. Ibid.

10. Susan O'Neill, *Don't Mean Nothing: Short Stories of Vietnam* (New York: Ballantine Books, 2001), xii.

Chapter Six

1. Diane Sebek, telephone interview, April 17, 2003.
2. Ibid.
3. Ibid.
4. Ibid.
5. Ibid.
6. Ibid.
7. Ibid.
8. Ibid.
9. Ibid.
10. James S. Olson and Randy Roberts, *My Lai: A Brief History with Documents* (Boston: Bedford Books, 1998), p. 175.
11. Sebek.
12. Ibid.
13. Ibid.

Chapter Seven

1. Ron Steinman, *Women in Vietnam: The Oral History* (New York: TV Books, 2000), p. 230.
2. Karen Zeinhert, *The Valiant Women of the Vietnam War* (Brookfield, CT: The Millbrook Press, 2000), p. 40.
3. Ron Steinman, *Inside Television's First War* (Columbia, MO: University of Missouri Press, 2002), p. 45.
4. Patience Mason, telephone interview, April 14, 2003.
5. Lorry M. Fenner and Marie E. de Young, *Women in Combat: Civic Duty or Military Liability* (Washington, DC: Georgetown University Press, 2001), p. 132.
6. Fenner and de Young, p. 166.
7. Ibid., p. 6.

Index

About the Author

Amanda Ferguson writes and teaches in Los Angeles.

Photo Credits

Front cover, pp. 13, 21, 22, 25 © AP/Wide World Photos; back cover © Pete Saloutos/Corbis; p. 6 © Genevieve Naylor/Corbis; pp. 8, 30, 39, 50, 80 © Hulton Archive/Getty Images; pp. 11, 34, 36, 61 © Bettmann/Corbis; p. 14 © Bohemian Nomad Picturemakers/Corbis; p. 28 © Corbis; p. 42 © Marcy Nighswander/AP/Wide World Photos; p. 44 © Bruce Burkhardt/Corbis; p. 55 © AFP/Corbis; pp. 49, 65 Still Picture Branch, National Archives and Records Administration; p. 70 US Naval Historical Center; p. 75 © Everett Collection, Inc.; p. 82 courtesy of Janet (Small) Woods; p. 83 Wisconsin Historical Society (1943); p. 89 © Jacques Langevin/Corbis Sygma.

Designer: Evelyn Horovicz; **Editor:** Mark Beyer; **Photo Researcher:** Peter Tomlinson